PASTOR JOKES

Christian Puns and Jokes
to Charm a Church,
Laugh with Friends,
& Ease the Soul

Stephen Fide

Bon Roi Press

To:

From:

A bible verse for you:

A message for you:

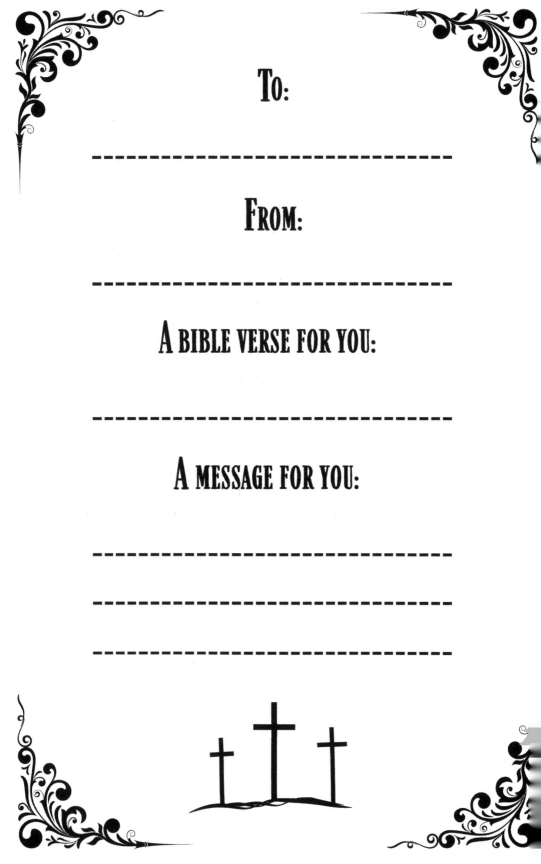

THEN WAS OUR MOUTH FILLED
WITH LAUGHTER, AND OUR
TONGUE WITH SINGING...

PSALM 126:2

Q: Why wasn't Lot's wife
invited to dinner parties?

A: Because she was a pillar
of salt.

Q: Why did Samson break
up with Delilah?

A: Because their relationship
was built on shear deception.

Q: What did Apostle Thomas say about the chicken crossing the road?

A: I doubt it.

Q: What does it mean when a laundromat is next to a church?

A: Cleanliness is next to godliness.

Q: What kind of car would
Jesus drive?

A: A Christler.

Q: When do some people only
go to church?

A: When six strong men carry
them there.

Q: Why couldn't Noah play cards on his ark?

A: Because he was standing on the deck.

Q: Why shouldn't Christians tell secrets in church?

A: Because someone is bound to pass the Word around.

Q: What did the Israelite say when someone served them pork?

A: Oh my lard!

Q: To keep slim, do you run daily?

A: No, but I do walk with the Lord daily.

Q: How do you make
holy water?

A: You boil the hell out of it.

Doubters: Jesus is the Son of
God? No way.

Christians: Yahweh!

An atheist man sat down to wait for his appointment. Having a bad day, he yelled aloud, "There is no God nor afterlife." The little girl next to him stopped reading her book, and asked, "Question: horses, cows, and deer all eat grass. Yet deer excrete pellets, cows a flat patty, and horses clumps. Why do you think that is?" The man was surprised by her intellect: "I don't know." She replied, "Do you feel confident to claim there's no God nor afterlife when you don't know poop?"

Q: How did Adam explain to his kids why he no longer lives in Eden?

A: "Your mother ate us out of house and home."

Q: How does an Israelite make tea?

A: Hebrews it.

Ann: Jones is struggling with money. He's just a poor preacher.

Brian: I know, I hear him every Sunday.

Q: In the Bible, who had no parents?

A: Joshua, son of Nun.

The Sadducees don't believe in the resurrection of the dead. That's why they're sad, you see.

Q: Why do people get full so easily at church potlucks?

A: They're amateurs.

A priest, a rabbi, and a bishop all walk into a bar. The bartender goes, what is this, a joke?

Mike said that God predestined him to sleep in this morning. Mike also said he was predestined to enjoy three Big Macs and an ice cream later.

If God is your co-pilot - Well, maybe you should swap seats!

Jesus said to a man, "Come forth, and win eternal life."

But the man came fifth and won a toaster.

Pastor: Lord, without you we are but dust.

Child: Mommy, what is butt dust?

Q: If it wasn't the apple that caused trouble in Eden, what was it?

A: It was the pair on the ground.

A little boy thought he was allowed to have 16 wives. A pastor asked him why. The boy replied, count them: 4 better, 4 worse, 4 richer, 4 poorer.

Q: How can our Lord and Savior afford to pay for all of our sins?

A: Jesus saves.

The doctor who delivered
Abraham's baby had a lisp.
"Is it a girl?" Abraham asked.
"No, Ishmael,"
the doctor replied.

Jesus is divine, and we are
di-branches (John 15:5).

Goliath used to be a great warrior. But that was before David rocked his world.

Q: Why did Jesus go to a Japanese restaurant with me?

A: Because he loves miso.

Blind Isaac: Essau! Come, I have to bless you before I kick the bucket.

Jacob: Here I am (hehe).

Isaac: You're Essau?

Jacob: Ya.

Isaac: Are you sure?

Jacob: Very.

Isaac: You do smell like Essau... but your voice, it's like Ja-

Jacob: It's in your head. Hurry up and bless me!

Q: Who knew the most people in the Bible?

A: Not sure, but Abraham surely knew a Lot.

The oldest computer in Eden was an apple. With only one byte, everything crashed.

Q: Why did Baal's followers believe in the false god?

A: They thought he could baal them out.

A man runs fast from the clutches of a lion. He prays, "Lord, please make this lion a Christian!" The lion then prays, "Dear Lord, thank you for this meal I'm about to receive."

Q: What kind of lights did
Noah use on the ark?

A: Flood lights.

Q: Why can't Jesus wear
jewelry?

A: He breaks every chain.

Q: When people dine with King Solomon, why is it hard for them to give up?

A: Solomon seats them at his ban-quitting table.

Q: How can you tell that Job was an introvert?

A: He only had three friends.

Q: Why did the Caananites
hate math?

A: When they tried to multiply,
Israel divided their land.

Q: Why didn't Pharaoh trust
his barber?

A: Everytime Pharaoh asked
for a trim, he was *plagued* with
a bad haircut.

God: Cain, where is your
brother?

Cain: He wasn't Abel to make
it. Ba dum tss.

Eve: Adam, are you cheating
on me?

Adam: I'm definitely not.
Count my ribs.

Q: What did Lot say to his wife
as they escaped Sodom?

A: "Hey, are we being
followed?"

Q: Who were the hottest guys
in the Bible?

A: Shadrach, Meshak, and
Abednego.

Jesus: You should forgive people who have done you wrong.

The world: Sounds good! ...But what if they-

Jesus: Did I stutter?

Q: How do we know the Magi were wise men?

A: They brought gold, myrrh, and some frickin' sense.

Q: Why was Abraham going to sacrifice Isaac as a child?

A: Because if Isaac were a teenager, it wouldn't have been a sacrifice.

Q: Why did Peter deny Jesus?

A: Because He healed Peter's mother-in-law.

Q: Why couldn't Noah go
fishing on the ark?

A: There were only two worms.

Q: What do you call Batman
when he skips church?

A: Christian Bale.

Q: What happened when Jesus cast demons into a herd of pigs?

A: He made the world's first deviled ham.

Q: Who were the acrobats in the Bible?

A: The Philippians.

Q: What is a spy's least favorite book in the Bible?

A: Dude-they're-onto-me.

-Lot having dinner with guests-

Guest: Lot, what ever happened to your wife?

Lot: Let's just say she was *assaulted.* Can someone pass the wif- I mean salt?

A devout man was caught in a flood. A boat arrived to rescue him, but he selflessly said, "Go rescue others! God will save me." Another boat came. The man told it the same thing. The rising water forced him onto a church roof. A helicopter came, but the man waved it away again. Finally, he was overcome by the waves. In Heaven, the man was reunited with his wife. He asked, "Why didn't God save me?" She said, "Are you not in Heaven? AND He sent two boats and a helicopter!"

Q: What do you get when you mix a Jehovah's witness with an agnostic?

A: Someone who doesn't know why they knocked on your door.

Non-Christians don't recognize Jesus, Protestants don't recognize the Pope, and Baptists don't recognize each other in a liquor store.

Q: Why did many Israelites ask Jael for a place to stay?

A: Because her hospitality was killer.

If Mary had Jesus, and Jesus is the Lamb of God, does that mean Mary had a little lamb?

Q: Why did an unemployed man get excited while sifting through the Bible?

A: He thought he saw a Job somewhere.

I have a joke about King Herod, and baby, it's killer!

Is it hot in here? Or is it the Holy Spirit burning inside of me?

Q: What vehicle is most likely to be Christian?

A: A convertible.

Q: What do you call a priest
who becomes an attorney?

A: A father-in-law.

A child didn't feel like doing
the dishes, so he introduced
them to Christ. Now they've all
been washed clean.

Q: Why do hurricanes restore school-aged kids' faith in Jesus?

A: Because when school is closed, they think, "There is a God!"

Singles should want their future husband/ wife to be the same as their Word document: saved.

Q: What should you say to invite your friends and family to church?

A: Come with me if you want to live.

Q: What does a church and an ice cream shop have in common?

A: They both have great sundaes.

Everyone's goal should be
to remember Bible verses better
than they can remember why
they walked into the kitchen.

Q: Which biblical king liked to
do things on his own?

A: Solomon.

Ticket booth: Sir, why did you buy a discounted ticket for kids, not adults?

Man: Because I'm a child of God...

An artist was selling her portrait of Elijah. You could say she made a prophet.

A father and his little boy listen to a sermon in church. Suddenly, the boy feels ill. His father tells him to run behind the church and throw up in the bushes. The boy bolts for the door and is about to exit when something catches his eye. He makes a beeline for a box and fills its contents with vomit. He returns to his father. "Did you throw up?" the father asks. "Yes," the boy responds. "But I didn't have to go to the back. There was a box by the door that said "For the sick."

Q: What does Carrie Underwood say when her expenses are too high?

A: Jesus take the bills.

The Lord moves in mysterious ways, but you don't have to. Use your turning signal.

Q: What did Peter say to Judas at Thanksgiving?

A: Judas you should carve the turkey since you're so good at stabbing things in the back.

Q: Where did Noah keep his bees?

A: In the archives.

Q: How full of Christ should Christians want to be?

A: So full that if a mosquito bites you, it flies away singing "There is power in the blood!"

Q: How do you hide sin from God?

A: You don't. It's like trying to hide behind a pole.

Q: What would a Christian
insurance gecko say?

A: Millions of people can
be saved by switching over
to Jesus Christ.

Q: How can a man ask for a
Christian lady's number?

A: "I was reading the book of
Numbers last night. Then I
realized I don't have yours."

If you ever get caught sleeping at work, here's what you do: Slowly raise your head and say "In Jesus' name I pray, amen."

Q: A man went on a scale to check his body weight. What did he find?

A: That the armor of God is quite heavy.

Christian: Not today, Satan!

Satan: Ok...

...What about tomorrow?

Q: What is like an unsharpened pencil?

A: Life without Lord God.
There is no point.

Q: What verse did the mom tell her little boy who kept dirting the toilet seat?

A: "...Aim for perfection... And the love of God and peace will be with you." (2 Corin. 13:11)

Church is not full of sinners. There is always room for more (Romans 3:10).

Q: If you hit a donkey three
times, what would happen?

A: It would say, "What did I do
for you to hit me three times?"
(Numbers 22:28)

Q: Does the king of Rock and
Roll still live?

A: No, but the King of Kings
does.

Q: What can a Christian say to improve their self-esteem?

A: I may not be all that, but Christ thinks I'm to die for.

Q: How can you get your pastor to speak highly of you?

A: Give him some helium.

Q: What happened when King David lost his ID?

A: He became King Dav.

A man disputes charges with his credit card company. He keeps explaining that Jesus paid all of his debts, but they don't want to hear it.

A cop notices a black car swerving on the road. He asks the driver to pull over. When the cop looks through the driver's window, he notices a bottle in a brown bag. "Have you been drinking?" the cop asks. "No, why do you ask?" the driver responds. "The bottle over there, why is it in a bag?" The driver says, "Oh, it's just water." "Mind if I see?" the cop asks. "I don't mind," the driver replies. The cop takes a sip. "Sir, this is wine." The driver exclaims, "Praise the Lord, He's done it again!"

As Christians we're called
to live like we want to meet
Jesus, not drive like we want
to meet Him.

Q: For what reason did the girl
keep walking by the same
person in church?

A: They said we're supposed to
walk by Faith!

Q: How do you prevent your pastor from getting mad when your phone rings in church?

A: Set your ringtone to "Amen!"

Q: Why didn't Adam ask Cain to help him reap?

A: Because he was still not Abel.

Q: Which sin can turn your temple into a megachurch?

A: Gluttony.

Q: What are the benefits of a $500 fan?

Q: Not sure, but it better blow the Holy Spirit through the whole house for that price.

Cop: Which way are you headed?

Driver: To Heaven, God-willing. And which way are you headed?

Q: What do we all wonder during summertime?

A: Why didn't Noah swat the two mosquitoes?

Q: Do Christians get angry?

A: No, they just get a
little cross.

Q: Did it hurt when you fell
from Heaven?

A: Are you implying that I'm
Satan?

Q: What did Mary use to brew coffee?

A: Holy grounds and holy water.

Q: What was the positive side of getting kicked out of Eden according to Adam?

A: "At least my wife can't complain that I never listened to her."

Q: What was the positive side of getting kicked out of Eden according to Eve?

A: "I married what used to be the perfect man."

Q: Will stop, drop, and roll work in Hell?

A: Probably not.

The goal is to be the kind of Christian who, when your feet touch the ground in the morning, the Devil says, "Oh no, they're up!"

Peter: John, don't write it. Don't-

John: "So they ran both together: and the other disciple *did* outrun Peter, and came first to the tomb." (John 20:4)

Q: Why did the teacher want to see Matthew, Mark, Luke and John after class?

A: Your book reports are all so similar.

Q: What could be Jesus' jingle if He sold insurance?

A: Like a good savior Jesus is there. All your sins fully covered.

Q: Why were Lot and his wife arguing before escaping Sodom?

A: She was salty that they had to leave town.

Jesus drove a Honda, but didn't brag about it. "For I speak not of my own Accord" (John 12:49).

Q: How did the Lord teach us
how to do laundry?

A: In the beginning of time,
He separated the light from
the dark.

Q: Why was Noah upset with
the chicken in the ark?

A: They were using fowl
language.

Q: Who are the most excited
people in church?

A: Moms when the pastor
starts talking about disobedient
children.

Q: What kind of cellphone did
Delilah use?

A: A Samson.

Q: What should you do if you overeat during the holidays?

A: Rebuke the calories in the name of Jesus.

Q: Does a person have to go to church to go to Heaven?

A: No, you don't have to wear a parachute to jump out of an airplane. It helps though!

Q: What do Christian parents say when a boy wants to date their daughter?

A: Great! When are you going to pick us all up?

Q: Why didn't the workers at the tower of Babel finish their job?

A: They just couldn't get their message across.

A scientist successfully re-creates conditions for life to flourish in his lab. He believes he can produce single-celled organisms from scratch. Proud, he says to God, "I can do what you do." God chuckles and responds, "Can you? How about this: I'll create a little life here, and then you do the same. We'll compare." The scientist accepts. God combines some dirt and chemicals. They become single-celled life forms. The scientist, excited to do the same, then reaches for some dirt. But God interrupts, "Oh no. No, you get your own dirt."

Q: Why weren't two velociraptors on the ark that Noah built?

A: They thought the ark was leaving at 11:00, but it actually left at 10:30.

Q: Who was the most disappointed when the prodigal son came home?

A: The fatted calf.

Q: Which Bible character was very fit?

A: *Abs*alom.

Abraham used to tell a joke about Lot's wife. Looking back, it wasn't a great idea.

Q: How many will be in Heaven and how many will be in Hell?

A: Only God knows. But if there's a stairway to Heaven and a highway to Hell, that's a good clue!

Men should make coffee for their lady. It says so right in the Good Book: Hebrews.

Printed in Great Britain
by Amazon